How to Succeed with LinkedIn: Tips, Tricks and Connection Scripts Every LinkedIn Member Needs to Know

How to Succeed with LinkedIn: Tips, Tricks and Connection Scripts Every LinkedIn Member Needs to Know

By Philip Calvert

First Edition: 2019

ISBN: 978-1-696-19636-9

www.philipcalvert.com

Contents

Introduction

I've been using LinkedIn since the beginning. And before that I used a website called Ecademy.com – believed to be the world's first B2B social networking site.

Ecademy started in 1998 and for many years did much the same as LinkedIn does now, so they were way ahead of their time.

Unfortunately, in many ways they were a victim of their own success, and when LinkedIn and others came along with far bigger budgets for development and growth, Ecademy sadly disappeared.

But many of the people I met on Ecademy, are active today on LinkedIn - many of whom happily reminisce about those early days of online social networking.

I first discovered Ecademy in 2002 as a recently new entrant to the world of self-employment, and to discover a website where I could 'meet' people online and refer them and their services to others without the need to exchange business cards in the flesh was a revelation.

That's not to suggest that face to face networking isn't important. In fact, it's more important than ever. But what many people forget (or perhaps do not fully appreciate) is that social networking sites are NOT a shortcut for building robust business relationships.

The most successful users of LinkedIn realise and know that the site is a conduit for discovery and for facilitating conversations that can later build to business. At its heart, LinkedIn is a search engine – the people search engine.

Many users think that just having a profile on LinkedIn will be sufficient, and that all the norms of fostering trust, credibility and relationships can be neatly side-tracked. Unfortunately, that is not the case. Successful networking online has nothing to do with the technology – it's about technique.

In this short guide I have tried to get to the heart of what LinkedIn is all about and how you can use it to attract more of the clients and connections that you really want.

Hopefully you'll find it to be an easy read, with proven tips, tricks and strategies that you can take away and implement in your business straight away.

Forty-Eight Reasons to Use LinkedIn

Whilst every internet marketer shouts about the awesome power of Facebook to drive traffic, attract leads and to win new clients and customers, sitting quietly behind the scenes is another lead generating monster...

The truth is, most people look at LinkedIn and wonder what the fuss is all about.

Whenever I speak at a conference or event, I always ask the audience to let me know if they are on LinkedIn – and almost everyone puts up their hand.

But when I then ask who knows *why* they are on LinkedIn, hardly anyone puts up their hand!

So, why are we all on LinkedIn if we don't know what we're doing there?

It's simple. Herd mentality has a lot to do with it.

And probably someone once told you that you *need* to be on LinkedIn.

Everyone else is on there, so I better be on there too...

True, you might well be looking for a job, in which case you have an obvious reason to be on LinkedIn.

And there's the clue – if you are going to get the best out of the platform, you need to have a clear reason for being there.

There could be many reasons why you are on LinkedIn. Here are forty-eight to get you started!

1. To look for a new job
2. To learn about companies where you might want to work
3. To post job opportunities
4. To build a new career
5. To build your personal brand
6. To build trust and reputation
7. To establish credibility
8. To help you appear in Google search results
9. To attract new clients and customers
10. To share your knowledge and expertise with others
11. To network with fellow professionals and those outside your immediate network

12. To re-connect with friends from school or college
13. To stay up to date on what's happening within your network
14. To follow thought leaders
15. To position yourself as an expert or thought leader
16. To follow certain companies and organisations
17. To increase the visibility of your communications
18. To attract leads
19. To drive traffic to your website
20. To build your newsletter list
21. To reach out to, and engage with influencers in your market
22. To sell your products and services
23. To find distributors, providers and suppliers
24. To find joint venture partners
25. To build community around your brand
26. To share announcements from your company
27. To help employees to become brand ambassadors
28. To help your company to differentiate itself from your competition
29. To join special interest groups

30. To get answers and solutions to problems
31. To teach staff and colleagues how to use social media more effectively in business
32. To help your CEO and leadership team to become 'social leaders'
33. To share your seminar or sales PowerPoint presentations
34. To meet journalists and increase media mentions
35. To highlight your skills
36. To highlight your work or business achievements
37. To highlight awards that you have won
38. To highlight your books and publications
39. To highlight your volunteer experience
40. To find a mentor
41. To make yourself available as a mentor
42. To publish testimonials
43. To get endorsements for your skills
44. To connect with people who have similar interests
45. To see who is following your updates or who has viewed your profile
46. To discover how your salary compares with others with the same expertise
47. To learn new skills

48. To find service providers for a project (not available globally)
49. And much more...!

The key thing is not to be a passive bystander on LinkedIn.

If you're going to have a presence there, then you will get so much more out of it if you have a clearly defined reason and a plan for how you are going to use it.

If you don't, you'll end up being one of those people who says:

"I don't get LinkedIn"

or

"I'm fed up with strangers wanting to connect with me"

or

"There are too many spammers".

In other words, you can't see the wood for the trees.

At the end of the day, LinkedIn is a piece of software, and like all software, unless you take time to learn how to use it, you will most likely never really benefit from it.

Take control of your LinkedIn membership and let's get started...

Top 21 'Must Do' Action Points for Winning with LinkedIn & Attracting More of the Clients and Contacts you Really Want

#1 Have A Clear Plan

As said above, sit down and brainstorm WHY you are on LinkedIn and what you want to get out of it. Literally write down some goals for your use of the site. Take a moment right now to come up with up to five goals:

1.

2.

3.

4.

5.

Once you know your goals, write them down and pin them on the wall in front of you.

Once you know *why* you are on LinkedIn, your experience of the platform will be transformed as you will have a renewed sense of purpose and focus.

#2 Fully Complete Your Profile

And I mean FULLY complete your profile...

Go through every single section and fill it out in detail. Don't skimp on this; time spent on this now will bring big rewards later.

Why spend so much time on completing my profile?

Because LinkedIn rewards profiles that are fully completed by putting them higher in search results. It also gives people a better experience when they visit your profile. A half-completed profile always creates a lacklustre impression on the reader.

Plus, when you fully complete your profile, it increases the likelihood that your LinkedIn profile will appear in search results when someone Googles your name.

#3 Keywords

As part of fully completing your profile, write down a list of a dozen keywords that sum up your area of expertise.

A 'keyword' can also be a very short phrase such as 'Financial Planning' or 'Internet Marketing'.

Then, put your list of keywords in order of importance, with the most important keywords at the top of the list.

Then, take the top five keywords on your list and add some or all of them into every section of your profile. Use the remaining keywords as appropriate throughout your profile.

When you take the time to use your top keywords into carefully thought-through text, this will make an immediate improvement to your visibility on LinkedIn.

Pro Tip: Edit/customise your LinkedIn profile URL to include an important keyword. At the very least, edit your URL to show just your name, rather than the jumble of name and random numbers/letters that LinkedIn gives you.

But consider replacing your name altogether like I have done. Note that I have replaced my name with just keywords:

www.linkedin.com/in/saleskeynotespeaker

By doing this, I am increasing my chances of being found by a conference organiser who is looking for a sales speaker.

Note that this is an advanced technique, so think it through carefully before doing something like this with your profile URL.

Bonus Tip: Fully completing your profile also means including your location. Both recruiters and people looking to hire consultants, trainers and coaches often search by location, so if you don't include it, you may well miss out.

According to LinkedIn, adding your location makes you 23 times more likely to be found in LinkedIn searches...

Also, when you are choosing your keywords, consider adding:

Keywords related to the services you offer:

- Telecoms
- Customer Service
- Financial Planning
- Coaching
- Etc.

Keywords related to your technical skills:

- Platforms
- Tools
- Certifications
- Languages
- Data analysis
- Project management
- Software languages etc.

Keywords related to industries you serve:

- Healthcare
- Law
- Manufacturing
- Travel

- Food and beverage
- Accounting etc.

Keywords related to target Industry buzzwords:

- For example, DB, SIPP, PHI, FCA in UK Financial Services

Keywords related to your business skills:

- Leadership
- Project management
- Strategy
- Customer service
- Presentations
- Sales etc.

Keywords that are geographical locations you target, for example:

- New York
- London
- Sydney etc.

You may also want to consider including keywords related to niches or special interests that you have:

- Fishing
- Fine wine
- Fitness
- Art

#4 Your Photo

You MUST have a profile photo. If you don't, you might as well cancel your LinkedIn account.

Really, leave now if you have no intention of having a photo, because countless studies have shown that people just aren't interested if you don't have one.

Make sure that your photo is friendly, professional and makes you look trustworthy. Avoid anything too 'corporate', but equally don't have a photo of you looking too casual – like in your swimming costume on the beach...

And don't use a picture of Batman or James Bond or your dog. Yes, I've seen plenty of those on LinkedIn.

Similarly, don't upload your logo instead of a photo. Many people do that, but it dramatically reduces the number of people who will connect with you because the perception is that it is spammy. Remember, people buy people.

Also, make sure that your photo is high resolution with a file size up to 8MB. People visiting profiles often click on the photo, so make sure they get to see a great photo of you that is not grainy.

#5 Your Cover Photo

Regardless of whether you have standard or premium membership of LinkedIn, you should upload a cover photo. That's the big image at the top of your profile.

Where possible, use an image that reflects something related to your expertise, skills and target market. For example, if you look at my cover photo, you can see a photo of me speaking on a large stage.

www.linkedin.com/in/saleskeynotespeaker

If you use an image editing software tool like Canva, you can also overlay some text to add emphasis to what you want to say.

#6 Add Photos and Media Throughout Your Profile

This is the sixth tip, and three of them have been about photos.

What does that tell you?

Add photos, videos, presentations, PDFs, infographics throughout the about/summary and experience sections. Not everyone wants to read the carefully crafted text on your profile, and some would rather look at pictures. LinkedIn allows a lot of images now, so make the most of this feature.

There is also evidence to suggest that when you add media to your profile, it can help with your visibility on the site and thus increase profile views. I certainly saw a BIG jump in views after I added media to my own profile.

#7 Remember Mobile Visitors

One of your best friends when completing your LinkedIn profile is the 'return' key.

Use it to keep sentences on your profile short and also use bullet points to aid clarity.

Not only does this make your profile generally easier to read, but it is particularly helpful to the growing number of people who view LinkedIn on a mobile device.

After initial criticism of LinkedIn's mobile app, they have since put in a lot of work upgrading it – and whilst it is not perfect, its use is growing rapidly amongst LinkedIn's membership. In fact, there are some LinkedIn features which can currently only be accessed through the mobile app.

#8 'Experience' Isn't Necessarily Your Previous Job

Most LinkedIn members assume that the Experience section is where you list previous jobs and roles that you've held.

It is, but you can list *anything* in this section.

So perhaps as part of your job or business, you are hosting a webinar. You can list this in your

Experience section as a current *activity*. This section is not just for your current job.

Equally, if you ran a series of seminars in your region last summer, you could also add this to your experience section. Whilst they may not have been your actual job, they were an activity as *part* of your job, so can be listed in this section.

For example, on my own profile, my current job is listed as Professional Speaker. But I can also add additional entries listing individual speaking engagements.

How does this help?

It shows that you are active and busy, have value to share – and it helps you to appear in search results when you include some of your keywords.

#9 List Your Skills

Don't be shy, use the Skills and Endorsements section to highlight and show off all the areas where you have skills. Visitors to your profile can give you a one-click endorsement.

My personal view is that this feature is a bit clunky, but it's there and you should use it.

Make sure that you include some of your top keywords as skills that you list, because this also helps to influence where you appear in LinkedIn search results.

LinkedIn organises your skills as follows:

- Top skills
- Industry knowledge
- Tools & Technologies
- Interpersonal
- Other

'Other' doesn't have to be work related skills, so show another side of you by including skills like playing the guitar, advanced driving or perhaps watercolour painting etc.

Pro Tip: Technical skills aren't everything - when listing your skills, remember to include your SOFT skills too. Hiring managers report that they often find it hard to find people who are 'collaborative', 'adaptable', etc., simply because LinkedIn members don't include these on their profile.

Periodically, LinkedIn releases a list of the most over-used buzzwords on LinkedIn profiles. Here's the latest list:

- Creative
- Organisational
- Effective
- Extensive experience
- Track record
- Strategic
- Proven sales professional
- Leadership
- Dynamic
- Motivated
- Innovative
- Passionate
- Problem solving
- Expert
- Exceptional communication skills

What do you notice about this list?

That's right, they look like words you would find on a CV. The problem is, a huge proportion of the LinkedIn membership use words like this in the body of their profile and within the skills section, and as a result find it difficult to stand out from the crowd.

This is another reason to think very carefully about the words and phrases you use on your profile, so that they speak clearly and directly to either your dream connection/client or to your target market.

#10 Join Groups

For many people, Groups are the best thing about LinkedIn, because it's here where you can meet, interact and engage with people who have similar interests to you.

These can be work related interests or personal interests that you have. So, for example, if you are into (say) cycling, you will find over 670 groups on LinkedIn that are related to cycling.

These vary from general cycling enthusiasts through to cycling science, cycling jobs, local cycling groups, cycling press, folding bikes enthusiasts and so on.

If you work in the world of cycling, these groups create amazing opportunities to network with others in that field, build relationships, highlight relevant expertise and even grow your list.

Avoid trying to sell within these groups, because nobody welcomes it. You might even get kicked out. Simply use the group to draw attention to yourself and your profile through your 'likes', comments and the value you add.

Equally if you cycle for fun and fitness, again you will pick up a wealth of information and tips in these groups.

Having something in common with others is key in business and makes it far easier to build relationships that could lead to doing business together.

#11 Start Your Own Group

Starting your own group on LinkedIn is a big step, but one that can reap many rewards for you over time.

They are another way to build your list – and even if that does not involve acquiring an actual email address, it does mean that you have a group of people who will give you their undivided attention.

The more niche your group is, and the more value that you can add, the better.

Treat your group a bit like a fish tank, where the members are the fish. Of course, your fish need feeding every day, so make sure that you add valuable tips, ideas, resources and links (ideally) on a daily basis.

The more great content you post, the more people will want to join and the more engagement there will be. And in turn, the more people will be intrigued by who you are and will want to connect with you.

Although you do not have email addresses for the members of your group*, you can send members an occasional message by highlighting a post of interest. So, you could write a short newsletter as a post in your group and then click a button that will highlight it to members.

Members of your group can also get regular summaries of content in your group, and again LinkedIn will deliver this on your behalf - so make sure that you have added enough content to 'feed' everyone.

Once your group is properly established (and only you will know when that is), you can also OCCASIONALLY make members of your group a direct offer on one of your products and services.

I say 'occasionally' because, however good the content is in your group, you will annoy members if you are constantly promoting and selling stuff.

The idea is to, over time build a reputation for being someone who gives free value – and lots of it. Once that is established, only then should you consider including promotional messages.

It is a difficult balance to get right, but when you do, you will find your conversion rates are extremely high when you do promote an offer. Webinars (free and chargeable) are a great way to take members of your group further up your value ladder.

Groups also have an 'About This Group' tab, so again you can use this any way you wish, though I recommend that you use it to include keywords that are relevant to the group's content, so that it appears in search results.

Finally, a well-run group with great content is a fantastic and proven way to build community around your brand. I have also found that once you have a thriving group, it will inevitably send traffic to your own website when you get the message right.

*There are of course several ways that you can get email addresses for members of your group and drive traffic to your website, and I cover this in my one-to-one Skype/Zoom coaching sessions.

#12 Post Status Updates

At the top of the LinkedIn home page, you'll see a box that currently says, 'Start a post'. That's the status update box.

What most people do is to post slightly bland content that one way or another links back to their website or company page on LinkedIn. Or they will re-post something similar that someone else has posted.

The worst type of status update says something like:

Check out our latest blog on our website. Click here... [LINK]

So, it's no surprise that these posts receive very little engagement and are unlikely to result in someone being inspired to look closely at your profile page.

Whilst I'm not advocating that you post cat videos on LinkedIn as if it was Facebook, it is important to get people's attention in their news feed.

The secret to great status update posts on LinkedIn which get high views and engagement, is to tell short observational stories about something that that has recently happened in your life or work that either you or others could benefit or learn from.

It could be about someone you met on a train and the conversation you had, or perhaps something strange that happened in a meeting – but ideally it needs to have a human – and thus emotional element.

Avoid including a link to somewhere else in your post, and also avoid including images.

That's right, do the opposite of what you would do on Facebook – do not include images. There is a reasonable amount of evidence to suggest that the LinkedIn algorithm is more favourable towards posts that do not include images – unless they are highly emotive and create high initial engagement. That said, the algorithm also seems to favour status updates that include images when the post has been made through the LinkedIn app on a mobile device.

The reason you should not include links, is because the LinkedIn algorithm does not like posts that encourage people to leave LinkedIn, and so your post is shown to far fewer people on the site.

If you must include a link, add your post to LinkedIn *without* the link, and then immediately go back to it, hit 'Edit' and then add in the link. This 'tricks' the LinkedIn algorithm and your post is shown to more people.

You can also add your link to the first comment, and that seems to be OK with the algorithm.

When your post includes human and emotional content, you will inevitably attract Likes and comments, so LinkedIn then shows your post to even more people. The more people who see your post, the greater the likelihood of people visiting your profile page.

Finally, aim to post a status update three times a week minimum. Ideally daily. Play around with posting at various times of day to see what gets the best response. You can also try adding the same post at different times of the day to see if that increases traction. In short, split test your posting times.

At first you might find posting so regularly quite challenging and struggle to think of things to post. But after a short while, you start to notice things that would be suitable as you go about your day. You might be crossing the street and suddenly notice something, so keep a note of anything that happens or that you spot which could be used in a post.

#13 Post Articles

When the article feature was first introduced on LinkedIn, users found that their content reached thousands of people. I know several people who have attracted speaking and consulting business straight off the back of an article they posted on LinkedIn.

One person I know posted an article at 08.30 am one morning, and by 11 am had five booked speaking engagements in their inbox.

However, things have changed.

Today, unless you are an 'influencer', your post will generally only reach thousands of people if it has highly emotional content and a killer title. Occasionally LinkedIn's editors will spot an interesting-looking article and give it a boost.

In short, most people who post an article on LinkedIn today will get limited engagement with it.

So why post articles on LinkedIn today?

Firstly, the articles you post will be visible on your LinkedIn profile, so this content adds to how people perceive you. You also get some stats, so you can see what type of content you are posting is getting the best response.

If one article gets a lot more engagement than others, take some time to look closely at it, and figure out how it was different. Then post more like that one.

But more importantly, when you post an article on LinkedIn, you have an option to copy a link to that article to groups that you either run or are a member of, thus extending its reach and potential visibility.

For example, one of my target markets is Financial Advisers & Financial Planners. So, I will post an article on LinkedIn and can then copy and post the link to it in all the groups where Financial Advisers hang out. This always results in people visiting my profile.

However, there is another way to use articles on LinkedIn which will not only enhance the perception of your expertise and credibility, but which will also get good volumes of views of your profile.

Essentially these are the places where you can post content on LinkedIn:

- Status updates
- Articles
- Company pages
- Showcase pages
- Comments on other people's posts
- Groups
- SlideShare
- Advertising

Status updates are intended for short content and clearly articles are for longer material. However, many people post shorter, lower quality content within articles, so LinkedIn has changed things to encourage high quality submissions within the latter.

For articles to do well, they need to be:

- Long form
- Detailed
- High quality
- In depth
- Analytical
- Research based
- Include unique insights

In addition:

- Write about news in your industry
- Write about timely topics
- Bring your unique expertise to the post that others can't
- Don't repeat what others are saying
- Give an opinion and provide precise arguments
- Support arguments with industry case studies conducted by credible persons

So, you can see from this that the article section is not for lighter weight content that would be more suitable as status updates.

Articles that go for quality will be favoured by the algorithm, but again human editors at LinkedIn can also give your content a boost. One little-known way to get their attention is to tweet to @LinkedInEditors and invite them to look over your content.

This doesn't always work, but if your article is of the highest quality, they may well take notice.

In short, posting articles on LinkedIn can be well worth it, as long as you are prepared to put in the effort.

#14 Use Hashtags

LinkedIn has reintroduced hashtags, and this can help people to find you when they are using the LinkedIn search tool.

When you post a status update or an article, always include a few relevant hashtags – particularly if those hashtags are also amongst your top keywords.

You can also search for specific hashtags, which will bring up all content that includes that hashtag. So, using the cycling example from earlier, I can search for #cycling and then engage with all relevant content where I can add something of value/interest.

This again draws attention to yourself without selling and sends people to your profile page.

LinkedIn is now rewarding members for engaging with content that includes hashtags, particularly topics where you share an interest with someone else.

Here's what you need to do:

- Search for a hashtag e.g. #Golf

- Save/follow the hashtag #Golf when the search results appear. When you do this, you are signalling to LinkedIn that Golf is a topic of interest to you.

- Scroll down the feed which now only shows content related to Golf.

- Occasionally like and comment on other people's Golf related posts – saying something like *"Great post John, thanks for sharing. #Golf"* or *"Useful post Sue – I'll try that technique next time I'm playing #Golf"*

- When you comment in this way, make sure that your post has at least five words – plus your hashtag

What's important to know, is that LinkedIn is now recognising that a huge amount of the content on its platform is made up of people simply broadcasting content and not engaging with one another.

So, they are trying to encourage users to engage with content and other people where they have mutual interests – in this case Golf. And when you do that, LinkedIn will reward you by making you and your content more visible.

#15 Know Your Numbers

An important thing about LinkedIn, is to get into a routine with it.

And something you need to do on Mondays is to go to your Notifications stream and look for the message from LinkedIn that says how many searches you appeared in this week.

Then click on the 'See all searches' button and look at your data. Firstly, if you are not appearing in many searches over the week, it means that you have not completed your profile in as much detail as you should, and that very likely you have not completed the keyword exercise.

Assuming you *are* appearing in search results, with up to and beyond a thousand searches during the week, look at the data and ask yourself if your target market is appearing, along with the keywords they searched. LinkedIn gives you all this data.

After you have done this for a few weeks, you'll get a sense for whether or not your profile is appearing in search results for your target market.

If not, tweak your profile, rewrite and keep testing until you are appearing in search results for your exact target audience. Use words and jargon in your profile that your target market uses.

So, for example, if your target market is (say) Accountants, but you are appearing in search results for Graphic Designers, it's likely that your profile needs a rethink.

Hopefully you are beginning to see why your choice of keywords is so important. In many ways, your choice of keywords drives your entire experience of LinkedIn.

#16 The Single Most Important Feature On LinkedIn...

Everything we have been talking about so far in this guide has been about behaving in a way on LinkedIn which draws attention to yourself – and specifically *to encourage visits to your profile*.

Everything you do on LinkedIn should be aimed at putting yourself in the best possible light in groups, posts and comments that will encourage people to want to take a closer look.

It's all about creating curiosity.

And here's the thing... no-one ever looks at your LinkedIn profile by accident. They always do it for a reason and on purpose. And it could be just pure curiosity – but that's the point; what we should try to do in all our actions on LinkedIn is to pique someone's curiosity.

The single most valuable feature on LinkedIn tells you whether or not you are succeeding in this mission...

It's the 'Who's Viewed Your Profile' tool, and you currently access it via your profile page.

Now just imagine that you knew the names and details of everyone who visits your website – would that be useful to you?

Yes, of course it would. And that's the wonderful thing about this tool because it shows you who, off their own back, decided to look at your profile.

This information is of course hugely valuable to you. But it's what you do with it that really matters.

Before that, it's worth pointing out that if you have a Basic (free) account on LinkedIn, you will see the five most recent viewers in the last ninety days. Yes, some of them might be in private mode, but if you look at the list every day, you'll be pretty well up to date with everyone who has looked at your profile.

When you have a Premium account, you get to see the details of **everyone** who has viewed your profile over the last ninety days (except those in private mode).

Again – know your numbers. What is this information telling you? Are the right people looking at your profile? If not, keep tweaking your profile and your activity on the site until your target audience starts showing up.

Many people ask me if Premium membership is worth having, often arguing that it's expensive for a lot of small business owners.

Clearly if you are an HR Director or have a similar 'big' role in an organisation, then Premium has its benefits. But for small business owners, having this one feature of being able to see the full list of your profile viewers makes Premium worth having.

That said, even knowing just the last five people who looked at your profile could be the difference between getting a job or not, making a valuable new connection or winning/losing a big new contract.

#17 Say Hello...!

So, people are visiting your profile page. That's great news! We're making progress...

And hopefully we are constantly tweaking our profile to make it as relevant as possible to our target audience. Any of the following could result in someone visiting your profile:

- Search result
- Status update seen
- Article seen
- Profile update
- Activity in a group seen
- Like, share or comment seen
- You looked at someone's profile
- You followed someone
- Comment on a company page
- Comment on a showcase page
- Promotion outside LinkedIn
- Google search result
- It's your birthday
- Job anniversary
- New job/role
- Promotion
- They follow a hashtag you used

Now what?

Someone once told me that 99% of LinkedIn users never bother to say 'hello' or 'thank you' to people who visit their profile. I don't know if that figure is correct, but in my own experience it is bang on.

Why is this important?

If people took the trouble to look at your profile, they did it for a reason, so let's try to find out and see where it leads us...

#18 Thank People Who Have Looked At Your Profile

We're going to look at scripts in more detail at the end of this guide, but in the meantime, here's the exact script that I use when following up after someone has looked at my profile; and I send it as a connection request if they are not already in my LinkedIn network:

"Hi [Name]...

Thanks for taking a look at my profile today – I hope you found something of interest...

Optional but recommended extra to build rapport >> *[I noticed that we're both in the XYZ Cycling group!]* or *[I see that we have mutual connections in Sue Smith and John Jones]*

Please do let me know if I can introduce you to anyone in my network – in the meantime it would be great to connect please.

Thanks in advance [Name]…

Phil"

A few things to note:

My success rate at connecting with people using that script is well in excess of 90%. Sometimes it's nearer 100%

I have clients who told me that they got amazing new customers *the very first time* they used this technique.

I don't follow up *everyone* who visits my profile – you should look through the list of your viewers and use common sense as to who might be worth following up.

For example, I'm a professional speaker, and if a meeting planner or conference organiser looks at my profile, I will definitely follow them up.

Now this is important…

Do NOT go into sales mode if your perfect/dream customer shows up. Remember, all they did was look at your profile, so what we're trying to do now is start a conversation; nothing else. Hopefully that conversation will lead to a coffee.

Note in my message that I offered to help to broaden their network by connecting them to someone in my own network. This is a GIVING activity and people welcome it even if they don't take up the offer.

Our message/communication must seek to GIVE, not TAKE or sell. You'll notice that there isn't the slightest hint of a sales message in my contact request.

Use the words *"Thanks in advance…"*. I have seen research that suggests these words (complete with the three dots), increases the likelihood of a favourable response.

Most important of all, ALWAYS customise the message with their name – ideally at the start and the end of the message.

When using their name at the start of the message, include the three dots "…" after their name. This encourages people to keep reading. Out of the corner of their eye, they will also see their name further down the message – again this will encourage people to keep reading.

#19 Connect With People You Have Found Through Search

Here's the script that I use when I want to connect with people that I have found on LinkedIn – perhaps through search, in a group or elsewhere:

"Hi [Name]…

I was excited to find your profile on LinkedIn today. I see that we have mutual connections in John Jones and Sue Smith, and it would be great to connect please.

Or, instead of having mutual connections:

I noticed that we're both in the XYZ Cycling group on LinkedIn! or I see that we [have something else in common] and it would be great to connect please.

Thanks in advance [Name]…

Phil"

Points to note:

Never connect with people through the Connect button in the 'People You May Know' section.

Yes, connect with them by all means, but only do it via the Connect button on their profile page, otherwise you won't be able to customise the message.

And again, you need to look at their profile first so that you can find something of interest that you have in common.

The secret with connecting is finding something that you have in common – however small.

My Dad told me that 'people buy people' and that's as true online as it is face to face, so always look for the human-interest connection – be it cycling (or whatever), mutual connections, location, group membership or something else. You can usually find something.

I once got a big speaking engagement simply because I had a mutual interest in kickboxing with someone I found on LinkedIn.

Yes, it works...

#20 Get Even More Profile Views – Pro Tip

It's a simple fact that the more people's profiles you look at, the more will look at yours. And that's good news, right?!

Yes, human nature has a part to play.

You can leverage this by either spending time searching for ideal customers and visiting their profiles - or as some people suggest automating it.

There are several tools available that will automate visits to profiles several hundred at a time, and even send connection requests.

This has advantages and some (big) disadvantages. The advantages are obvious, but the disadvantages can be as bad as getting kicked off LinkedIn or sin-binned for a period.

These automation tools can be extremely useful but must be used with a great deal of care. For starters, if you are on the free version of LinkedIn, there is a 'commercial use' limit which is designed to stop spammers, but also to encourage bone fide heavy users to pay. E.g. recruiters etc.

LinkedIn won't tell you what your commercial use limit is, so it is best to use such tools **very sparingly**. If you suddenly go from doing very few searches a week to several hundred a day, the LinkedIn system will pick you up, so if you do use this approach, build it up very gradually over several weeks.

Many LinkedIn heavy users like me, find occasional automation incredibly valuable – but don't tell me you haven't been warned...!

I tend to use an automation tool about once a month, if that – perhaps when I'm searching for a very specific type of person. The tool I use will visit the profiles for me and then I go into manual mode when people start looking at my profile.

I would advise against using automation tools to send connection requests (even personalised with names) because you run the risk of too many not accepting your request, which again could lead to LinkedIn blocking your account for a while. In short, always do connection messages manually as described in #18 and #19 above.

To summarise, automation tools occasionally have their place, but LinkedIn frowns upon it and will block your account or similar if you abuse the system – and there is evidence to suggest that they are getting much tougher.

I include this tip, because there are many people suggesting that you use automation tools – or offer to do it for you. In short, I am hearing more and more that this is not a good idea, so if you must use automation, do so with extreme care.

Bonus tip on automation:

However, whilst not strictly an automation tool, there is a ***fantastic*** service that I use called VERY FAST.

Rather than automate the sending of messages, VERY FAST significantly speeds up the time it takes to send *personalised* messages that you were going to send anyway.

Simply what it does, is to allow you to create a series of template messages that you might want to send to people. The tool also personalises the messages with their name.

So for example, you could create template messages for:

- Replying to people who want to connect with you
- Sending connection request messages to other people
- Sending messages to unconnected people who have looked at your profile
- Sending messages to people who you are already connected with who have looked at your profile
- Sending messages to people who have wished you Happy Birthday
- Sending messages to people who have congratulated you on a new job or role
- Sending your own messages of congratulations to other people
- Sending messages of thanks to people who have endorsed you for one of your listed skills
- Welcoming people who want to join your LinkedIn group
- Sending messages to someone you might want to interview or recruit
- Sending follow up messages to prospects
- Sending messages to direct people to your website, funnel, special offer or free download

- Etc.

You can also send template messages to specific types of people who have done any of the above. So for example, you could send different messages depending on certain niches in which you operate or target.

Perhaps you target (say) Accountants and Financial Advisers with your products or services, so you can create a personalised template, each with a slightly different message depending on their industry.

As at the time of writing, the service is still in Beta, but to date it has saved me many hours of time.

Prior to using it, I would create template messages on a Word document or similar, and then copy and paste a message into LinkedIn, remembering of course to personalise it.

With VERY FAST, the whole thing is done in the blink of an eye.

The site is to be found at https://getveryfast.com

Oh, and it's (currently) free...

#21 Remove Distractions (Such as Your Competitors) From Your Profile Page...

One of the problems with LinkedIn, is that they proactively encourage you to connect with people. That's not a problem in itself - it's just that one of the places where they do that is on your profile page!

Have you noticed that when you visit someone's profile page on LinkedIn, usually on the right side it says, 'People Also Viewed'. Now if you work for a larger company, the people in that list are more than likely to be your colleagues or people in other companies in similar roles to you - or with similar skills and experience.

This can cause you problems if you are a) hoping that a recruiter will contact you about possible job opportunities, and b) if you are self-employed or have your own business.

If you are looking for a job and have flagged that up on LinkedIn (there's a tool where you can alert recruiters to your availability), when recruiters or potential employers visit your profile, if they see a list on the right side that says 'People Also

Viewed', they know that these are people who have similar skills to you - and they may well include them in their search. The list might even distract them altogether from your profile!

Equally, if you are self-employed or have your own business, when someone visits your profile to check you out - the last thing you want them to see on your profile, is a list of people who have similar skills and expertise as you. In short, the people in the list on the right are more than likely to be your competitors!

The good news is that within your LinkedIn privacy settings, you can turn off this feature. And I strongly suggest that you do that!

Yes, your profile is all about YOU. Don't let people visiting your profile get distracted by others who they might be tempted to talk to first...

LinkedIn Connection Scripts

When using LinkedIn, it's important to remember that we are not looking to do business with someone straight off your LinkedIn profile. It's extremely unlikely that someone will find our profile and make an immediate request to purchase our products or services.

What we are aiming to do through LinkedIn messages, is little more than to start a conversation.

These scripts include proven copywriting techniques, so try to avoid altering them too much - but feel free to model and customise them to your proposed connection's interests.

When the conversation is going in the right direction, look to build the relationship off LinkedIn in the traditional way. I.e. on the phone, over coffee etc.

How to thank people who are not connections and who have looked at your profile

Hi John...

Thanks for taking a look at my profile page – I hope you found something of interest [?]

I noticed that we have some mutual connections, and it would be great to connect please.

Thanks in advance...

Philip

On the surface this looks like a very simple script, but there's more to it than meets the eye.

- Send this message as a connection request.

- Always use their name as it shows you are potentially not a spammer. What's more it's polite and will help with trust etc.

- Add "..." after their name, because this hints to them that there is more to follow.

- Say *"thank you"* because it's polite and everyone likes to be thanked. If you have a real-life store, it's always good to say thank you to people for stopping by.

- The "?" is optional.

- Always try to say something that shows/proves that you have something in common. This is immediately appealing to most people. Just having mutual connections will normally be sufficient, but if it's clear from their profile that they and you both play golf, then refer to that.

  If you have mutual connections within a specific industry, refer to that. E.g. *"I see that we have mutual connections in the Accountancy world"*

- Finish with *"Thanks in advance..."*. I have found by split testing over time, that this phrase dramatically increases the likelihood that they will reply (or accept your request).

Someone asked to connect with you: V1

Assuming that you want to accept their request:

Hi Sue...

Yes! I'm very happy to connect – thank you and I appreciate your interest. [Optional: Welcome to my network!]

Please let me know if I can connect you to anyone in my network.

Can I ask what prompted you to say hello?

Thanks in advance...

Philip

- 99% of these requests will not have been personalised but reply as if they had been.

- One of the most important parts of this is the statement *"Please let me know if I can connect you to anyone in my network"* because huge numbers of people go straight into sales mode at this point. So, what you should do is the exact opposite. You do this by offering to give them something of potentially very high value. i.e. a useful connection.

In reality, hardly anyone takes you up on this, but you are using the law of reciprocity to make it much more likely that they will give you something back – even if it is an exchange of messages – which is exactly what we want.

- Very often they will reply to the question *"Can I ask what prompted you to say hello?"* and I have attracted business on many occasions by asking it in this message.

Someone asked to connect with you: V2

Hi Michael...

Yes! I'm very happy to connect – thank you. I see that you are a [Financial Planner]?

The majority of my [financial services] connections have joined my private forum. Almost 2,000 of them use it to share useful resources and to make valuable connections – you should join us...

Financial Planners are joining here [www.facebook.com/groups/AdviserLifeTalk]. And it's free!

Thanks in advance...

Philip

This is a bit more advanced because we are using LinkedIn and your message as the top of your funnel – driving them to some value that is highly relevant to them.

This pre-supposes that your LinkedIn plan is deliberately set up to attract specific types of people you want to work with — in this case financial advisers.

You will also note that the message includes social proof *"Financial Planners are joining here"*, and this serves to make the offer even more attractive.

When financial advisers ask to connect with me on LinkedIn, almost 100% of them go on to join my group.

Note also the words *"It's free"*, which just make it a no-brainer for them to join.

Someone followed you (instead of connecting with you)

Hi Jim...

*Thank you! I appreciate you following my profile –
I hope you'll find something of interest. [Optional:
I see that we both are connected to John etc]*

*Please let me know if I can introduce you to
anyone in my network. Can I ask what prompted
you to follow my posts?*

Thanks in advance...

Philip

You want to connect with someone

Hi Peter...

I spotted you on LinkedIn today and noticed that we have mutual connections in the [Accountancy] world.

It would be great to connect please.

Thanks in advance...

Philip

Again, a really simple message using the techniques mentioned earlier. One of the key parts is the phrase *"I spotted you on LinkedIn"*, which suggests that you discovered them as a result of something *they did* on the site.

If you are able to personalise the message even further, then all the better. For example:

Hi Peter...

I spotted you on LinkedIn today and noticed that we have a mutual interest in [Yoga]! How often do you practice?

It would be great to connect please.

Thanks in advance...

Philip

Or:

Hi Mary...

It was great to meet you at the conference today and I just spotted you on LinkedIn. What did you think of today's event?

It would be great to connect please.

Thanks in advance...

Philip

When they accept your request

Hi again Maria...

Great! Thanks for connecting – I appreciate your interest.

If I can connect you to anyone in my network, please don't hesitate to ask.

- *I noticed your post about [topic] and it caught my attention.*
- *I see that you are also connected to [James Smith]*
- *I see that you are based in [Cambridge]. It must be great working there!*
- *I'm doing a bit of research at the moment for a project - what is the biggest issue that Financial Planners are struggling with right now? I'd be keen on your thoughts*

Thanks in advance...

Philip

The bulleted points are suggestions – pick one or write something that will engage with the person concerned.

Key points in LinkedIn connection messages

- Always use their name

- Try to find things that you have in common, and refer to them in your message

- Offer something valuable that they won't be expecting. E.g. an introduction to someone in your network

- Never try to sell anything

- When you do point them to something of yours, it MUST be high value, free and directly relevant to their world. Through social proof, highlight that other people like them have already taken action

- All we're doing is starting a conversation. We are NOT going anywhere near sales mode at this point. Save that for when the time is right and only you will know when that is.

By way of a practical example, financial advisers often tell me that they get a lot of recruiters wanting to connect with them, and whilst most are not interested in connecting with them, some have turned it round to their advantage with this message:

Hi Tim...

Thanks for taking a look at my profile today – I see that you are in Recruitment? Please let me know if there is anyone in my network that I could introduce you to.

In the meantime, recruiters are downloading our guide "Ten Easy Ways for Recruitment Professionals to Increase Their Income in Retirement". It's free!

Recruiters are downloading it at www.mywebsite.com

Thanks in advance...

Mary

So, in this example you can see several of the messaging elements coming together in one communication. Model and adapt it to your own target market. The more niche you can make it, the better.

Networking like a Pro: Networking questions that build relationships online and offline

I hope that you have found this short book of interest, but I wanted to finish by making a vital point, and that is to stress the fact that LinkedIn is about Social *Networking* and not Social *Media*. It's an important difference.

Yes, on the surface LinkedIn looks like Social Media, and yes, many people use it that way. But if you want success on the site, remember that it is fundamentally a tool to help people to network with each other.

The more that you use it to interact and engage with people in a professional and human way, the more value you and they will get from it.

But many people simply don't know how to network, believing that networking is about meeting people, exchanging business cards and asking for business.

The worst type of networkers are the people who arrive early at a networking event and put a business card on every chair, in the hope that someone will get in touch. This *isn't* networking.

The best type of networking is where you go out of your way to help other people through your own network of contacts, and without any expectation of anything in return.

I'm going to finish with three questions that I use in any networking situations, which have served me well over many years.

Instead of *"What do you do?"* ask *"What is your area of expertise?"*

Then ask, *"What are you working on in your business at the moment that you are really excited about?"*

Or *"What big projects are you working on [in your business] at the moment?"*

And then *"Who could I connect you to who could help you with that?"*

Or

"What additional expertise would be useful to you if I could introduce you to someone who could help [who could bring the project in faster, cheaper etc]?"

As you can see, these questions are all about the other person and not about you. Listen carefully to their answers and get back to them as quickly as possible with a connection from your network.

Even if you don't have someone that you could introduce them to, get back to them anyway and keep the relationship plates spinning for another day. Either way, they won't forget you and one day they may well reciprocate by referring you to someone else.

If you use LinkedIn in much the same way – i.e. to help people by introducing them to people you know, you will find your experience of the site dramatically enhanced.

That's it – I hope you found this useful…

There is of course a lot more to LinkedIn than we have been able to cover here, including Company Pages, Showcase Pages, ProFinder, Live Streaming Video and some of the Premium tools such as Navigator.

But what you have here is literally the cheat sheet to getting it right on LinkedIn – and you can see that almost all of this can be done without paying for Premium.

To say thank you for buying this **guide, I want to give you access to my private group LinkedIn Marketing Secrets** where you'll discover many more proven LinkedIn tips, tricks and strategies.

Join everyone at https://linkedin-marketing-secrets.mn.co

To help us spread the word about this guide, please consider giving it a five-star review on Amazon – it is very much appreciated. Thank you.

About the Author

Philip Calvert is a specialist in helping companies, entrepreneurs and businesspeople to leverage online professional networking as part of their sales, marketing and communication strategies.

Philip is in demand as a LinkedIn expert and speaks at conferences and events worldwide. Clients who Philip has worked with include University of Cambridge, Santander, Scottish Widows, Maserati, Canon, Fiat, Pfizer and many others. He is a Fellow of the UK Professional Speaking Association.

To book Philip to speak at your event visit www.philipcalvert.com or contact him at philip@philipcalvert.com

Disclaimer and Terms of Use

may affect the applicability or effectiveness of these techniques.

Any earnings or other results quoted, are based on our own and the testing of other marketers and are estimates of what we believe you could earn. There is no assurance you will do as well as stated in any examples and could be influenced by a variety of factors, not least of which include site functionality, work ethic and market conditions. If you rely upon any figures provided, you must accept the entire risk of not doing as well as the information provided.

All product names, logos and artwork mentioned in this book are copyrights of their respective owners. None of the owners have sponsored or endorsed this publication.

Philip Calvert is neither employed by or affiliated to LinkedIn in any way and is the author or this book as an independent marketing consultant and speaker.

While all attempts have been made to verify information provided, the author assumes no responsibility for errors, omissions or contrary interpretation on the subject matter herein. Any perceived slights of people or organisations are unintentional. The purchaser or reader of this publication assumes responsibility for the use of these materials and information.

No guarantees of income are made. The author reserves the right to make changes and assumes no responsibility or liability whatsoever on behalf of any purchaser or reader of these materials.

The purchaser and reader assume full responsibility for compliance and compliant use of the material in this book, as defined by their respective regulatory body if applicable. No guarantees are made by the author that any of the ideas presented in this book will be acceptable under the purchaser or reader's local compliance regime.

Your Notes

Printed in Poland
by Amazon Fulfillment
Poland Sp. z o.o., Wrocław

52566058R00051